Create Yourself...

an 'Experience' waiting just for you.

Dr. Dolores Seymour, Msc.D., Ph.D.

Lifetime Books, Inc.
Hollywood, Florida

Copyright © 1992 Dr. Dolores Seymour

This publication is designed to provide accurate and authoritative information in
regard to the subject matter covered. It is sold with the understanding that the
publisher is not engaged in rendering legal, accounting, or other professional
service. If legal advice or other assistance is required, the services of a competent
professional person should be sought. From a Declaration of Principle jointly
adopted by a Committee of the American Bar Association and a Committee of
Publishers.

LIFETIME BOOKS, INC.
2131 Hollywood Boulevard, Hollywood, FL 33020

ISBN 0-8119-8119-3   : $9.95

I would like to dedicate this book to my mother, whose encouragement and guidance in my early childhood was invaluable, and who taught me the importance of 'being involved'.

Contents

Foreword

Create Yourself... by Dr. Dolores Seymour is one of the most essential books in modern times, directing you, the reader, towards high achievements, both personal and emotional.

Create Yourself... is predominantly a 'what-to-do and how-to-do-it' book. In it you'll find the magic touch of Dr. Seymour as she guides you effortlessly toward positive behavior patterns, revealing an amazingly simple system of self-management.

Thousands of people from every walk of life have applied Dr. Seymour's techniques for a healthier, happier, positive lifestyle. Her nuts and bolts approach will teach you how to live the life you were meant to enjoy.

Be prepared, as you put this plan into action, for a changed lifestyle which will lead to greater possibilities for you, emotionally, physically, and spiritually.

Charles P. Earley, M.D.

WHAT TO EXPECT FROM THIS PROGRAM

What can you expect to derive from this Behavior Modification Program? Quite simply, it has been designed to give you a structured plan to follow, along with the tools necessary to put this plan into action. You will learn to use each tool individually, perhaps focusing on just that one tool for a week or so, as you discover its range of possibilities. Upon completion of this book, you will have a whole array of new skills to draw upon, using whatever is needed in any given situation.

What you will develop is an *awareness* of your behaviors, so as to distinguish automatic responses from chosen actions. As you become more and more in control of your life, you shall also become more and more in control of your options.

In addition, you will learn to take daily problems and turn them into challenges that can become golden opportunites. You will do this with the confidence of a true champion. You will know how to be who you

are and the best that you can be - and to be content
and satisfied with exactly that.

And please, don't place the cart before the horse...
don't wait to feel better before beginning this Behavior
Modification Program, but simply choose to begin
NOW. This is not unlike the overweight woman who
was encouraged to go swimming for exercise but
wanted to wait until she looked good in a bathing suit.
I think you get the point.

As you grow in awareness from applying these
techniques, you will treat your body, as well as your
mind and your spirit, with new respect, living each
day, each moment, to the fullest. You will discover
how to develop all of your senses: to hear, to smell, to
see, to feel, as well as to taste, with an added zest that
gives you so much more satisfaction than any of your
former, unhealthy choices.

I will ask you to think about things that may seem
totally unrelated to your physical and/or mental state;
they are, however, definitely relevant. You will begin
to really know yourself: as you are now - as you wish
to be - as you can be. I will show you how you are
limited only by your imagination, that you can achieve

whatever you can imagine!

Last, but certainly not least, you will learn to be content - with yourself and your life. If changes need to be made you will have the courage to make the necessary decisions for these changes.

Once you take your new skills and start using them you'll notice exciting transformations in the way people react to you and how you project self - confidence in any situation. A happier, healthier life can be yours with increased physical and mental energy, self-esteem, and, an inner peace that expands your understanding of YOU. My goal is to *exceed* your expectations - let this be your goal as well. And now, let's begin!

Who Are You

The first step is to become *aware* of who you are. Your name is but a convenient handle by which the world can call out to you or write to you - but seriously, *who* are you? When was the last time you stopped long enough to ask yourself this question? There are no right or wrong answers, this is simply to help you become *aware.*

And now, stretch a little, make yourself comfortable, take three, deep, relaxing breaths, and fill in the spaces below with whatever comes to mind first. Spend only one minute for each answer.

Who am I, as I am right now, this very moment?

List five:

1. I am_____

2. I am_____

3. I am_____

4. I am_____

5. I am_____

Who am I, as I wish to be?

List five:

1. I am_____

2. I am_____

Create Yourself...

3. I am_____

4. I am_____

5. I am_____

List ten benefits of being in control of your life:

1._____

2._____

3._____

4._____

5._____

6._____

7._____

8._____

Create Yourself...

9._____

10._____

BELIEVE IT OR NOT!!! (It doesn't matter...just do it.)

Mirror-Magic Exercise:

Go to your mirror, take a deep breath, look deeply into your eyes and say aloud, "I am wonderful! I am confident, and healthy, and satisfied in every way." Repeat this 3 times.

Your tone of voice should reflect calmness, strength, and confidence, in order to reinforce your message. If you wear glasses, remove them.

Note: If you should feel uncomfortable, take a deep breath and start again but always use eye contact.

Question: "Why do I have to say something that I don't believe because it's obviously untrue?

Answer: What you are doing in this exercise is consciously reprogramming your built-in computer by changing the automatic negative thoughts to automatic positive thoughts.

Example of negative thought and/or statement: "I don't care if one thousand others are confident and in control, I'm convinced that for me it's hopeless."

17

This negative thought reflects the kind of mental processing that is at the very core of your negative behavior patterns. Your negative thoughts, or interpretations, are one of the most frequently overlooked causes of negative habits and the following consequences. Your subconscious mind accepts whatever you say as truth - it does not analyze or dispute - it simply takes all the words and thoughts that you feed it, literally.

Example of positive thought and/or statement:

"I know I can do it!"

By learning to reprogram your computer, so to speak, you are restructuring your thoughts, and soon your habits will coincide with these positive thoughts. Therefore, if you consciously feed your subconscious mind positive messages, it will accept them as true and will proceed to bring them to reality as conditions, experiences, and events. Thus the phrase, "We create our own reality." And the truth is, we really do!

The habitual thoughts of your conscious mind establish deep grooves in your subconscious mind. Now this is great for you if your habitual thoughts are healthy, peaceful, and constructive. But - if you

18

indulge in worries or insecurities and other forms of destructive thinking, the result is obvious. Like attracts like: negative thoughts and statements attract negative results, postitive thoughts and statements attract positive results.

The solution to this stinkin' thinkin', as it is sometimes called, is evident. POSITIVE SELF-TALK! First, use the Mirror-Magic Exercise exactly as I have described twice daily for the rest of your life. It costs nothing and takes about 15 seconds of your time. Even when you are as you want to be, continue to do this for positive reinforcement. And, you'll have nothing but terrific side effects which include improved confidence, a positive outlook, and a healthy mind and body.

Next, use this same positive statement during the day at every opportunity, wherever you are and whatever you are doing. Say it for 5 minutes at a time, using your watch, either silently or aloud, and do this ten times daily for about three weeks at which time you will have created a positive habit. After three weeks of practice, it will become easier and easier to automatically remember to do your statement.

Choose to allow this to become part of your lifestyle. You can do it in the shower, while you're driving or watching television...you needn't concentrate, simply repeat it over and over.

Your greater power is your capacity to *choose* what you say and think. *CHOOSE* health - *CHOOSE* happiness - *CHOOSE* life! Remember, it doesn't matter whether or not you believe it, your subconscious doesn't know the difference, so - just do it!

FOR YOUR EYES ONLY...

Drawing is an expression of the psyche, bringing messages and symbols from your subconscious mind and even beyond, into your conscious mind and on your paper. Important - you needn't know how to draw at all! This is for your eyes only; your drawing will have meaning and understanding for *you*.

Because of the strong link between the psyche and soma, (mind and body) drawing can be a valuable, result producing pursuit as well as an excellent tool for discovering positive solutions to problem areas.

Directions For Image Page A:

What is your interpretation of what you are like now? Put yourself in this drawing, in a particular setting, using different colors and as many details as possible of what's around you as well as within you.

Note: Under your drawing, write your full name, including maiden name if woman, and nicknames if any.

21

Directions For Image Page B:

How do you want to look, ideally? Close your eyes, take several deep, relaxing breaths; inhale deeply and exhale just as deeply, as you repeat ten times, "I am wonderful! I am confident and content in every way." If you find it difficult to imagine yourself as confident and content, repeat this exercise over and over until you begin to think, imagine, or feel, how you want to be. Open your eyes and begin to draw again, this time as you want to be, ideally. As before, place yourself in an ideal setting which satisfies your every need, using as many details and colors as possible, with your full name at the bottom.

Create Yourself...

Image Page A

Create Yourself...

Image Page B

RECORD KEEPING *IS* FOR YOU!

In order to become aware, organized, and in control, it is important to keep records.

Record the percentage of effort, from 0% to 100%, that you have given to this entire program and compare this percentage to your results.

Week #1: % of Effort [   ]
   Are you more positive [ ], more negative [ ], the same [ ] ?
   Why do you think this happened?

   _____

   _____

Week #2: % of Effort [   ]
   Are you more positive [ ], more negative [ ], the same [ ] ?
   Why do you think this happened?

   _____

   _____

Week #3: % of Effort [   ]
   Are you more positive [ ], more negative [ ], the

25

same [ ] ?

Why do you think this happened?

_____

_____

Week #4: % of Effort [   ]

Are you more positive [ ], more negative [ ], the same [ ] ?

Why do you think this happened?

_____

_____

Week #5: % of Effort [   ]

Are you more positive [ ], more negative [ ], the same [ ] ?

Why do you think this happened?

_____

_____

Week #6: % of Effort [   ]

Are you more postitive [ ], more negative [ ], the same [ ] ?

Why so you think this happened?

_____

_____

Week #7: % of Effort [   ]

Are you more positive [ ], more negative [ ], the same [ ] ?

Why do you think this happened?

_____

_____

Week #8: % of Effort [   ]

Are you more positive [ ], more negative [ ], the same [ ] ?

Why do you think this happened?

_____

_____

Week #9: % of Effort [   ]

Are you more positive [ ], more negative [ ], the same [ ] ?

Why do you think this happened?

_____

_____

Week #10: % of Effort [   ]

Are you more positive [ ], more negative [ ], the same [ ] ?

Why do you think this happened?

_____

Week #11: % of Effort [   ]

Are you more positive [ ], more negative [ ], the same [ ] ?

Why do you think this happened?

_____

_____

Week #12: % of Effort [   ]

Are you more positive [ ], more negative [ ], the same [ ] ?

Why do you think this happened?

_____

_____

Week #13: % of Effort [   ]

Are you more positive [ ], more negative [ ], the same [ ] ?

Why do you think this happened?

_____

_____

Week #14: % of Effort [   ]

Are you more positive [ ], more negative [ ], the same [ ] ?

Why do you think this happened?

_____

Week #15: % of Effort [   ]

    Are you more positive [ ], more negative [ ], the same [ ] ?

    Why do you think this happened?

Week #16: % of Effort [   ]

    Are you more positive [ ], more negative [ ], the same [ ] ?

    Why do you think this happened?

LET GO OF STRESS ... ANYTIME

Let's do an exercise to release stress along with the negativity that accompanies it. This exercise costs nothing but a bit of time, something you can do while sitting or lying down with your eyes closed.

Imagery Exercise

Close your eyes and instruct your mind and body to relax. Inhale deeply and slowly through your nose, hold your breath for a count of five, then exhale through your mouth, thinking and imagining that you are letting go of all the stress and tension in your mind and your body. Allow your mind to be free and clear as you concentrate only on your breathing. Repeat this five times.

Now, breathe normally, slowly, and begin to count backward from ten to one, repeating each number as you exhale. When you reach the number one, mentally picture in your mind the most peaceful, comfortable, relaxing scene that you can posibly can. Picture your scene with as many details as possible:

the sounds, the colors, the smells - perhaps by a running brook with a waterfall nearby or - in a soft, green, grassy meadow with a beautiful, blue sky above or - on a deserted beach at sunset, with the waves rolling in and out and the seagulls gliding overhead.

Think about and imagine yourself in this scene completely relaxed and at peace...healthy, happy, confident, and content. Notice what you are wearing, the style, the colors. Appreciate how attractive you feel...how attractive you are. Stay here as long as you like, keeping the breathing calm and regular.

When you wish to end the exercise, take a deep breath, open your eyes, gently stretch your arms and your legs, and get up slowly.

Do this exercise twice daily, and more if you can, until you look in the mirror and see the reality you have created.

SELF-ANALYSIS

This is for your eyes only. Examine the following areas honestly, and develop a complete picture of yourself in detail. Write a brief paragraph on each of these aspects of your life.

Family History:_____

_____

_____

_____

_____

_____

Parents:_____

_____

_____

_____

_____

_____

Religious Background:_____

Create Yourself...

_____

_____

_____

_____

_____

Present Religious Beliefs:_____

_____

_____

_____

_____

_____

Childhood:_____

_____

_____

_____

_____

_____

Love:_____

_____

_____

33

Create Yourself...

_____

_____

_____

Spouse - Children:_____

_____

_____

_____

_____

Home Environment:_____

_____

_____

_____

_____

Entertainment:_____

_____

_____

_____

_____

Create Yourself...

_____

Nutrition:_____

_____

_____

_____

_____

Career:_____

_____

_____

_____

_____

Physical Exercise:_____

_____

_____

_____

_____

Create Yourself...

Social:_____

_____

_____

_____

_____

_____

Friends:_____

_____

_____

_____

_____

_____

Travel:_____

_____

_____

_____

_____

_____

Health:_____

_____

_____

_____

_____

_____

Hobbies:_____

_____

_____

_____

_____

_____

Study:_____

_____

_____

_____

_____

_____

Hooray! You know who and what you are. Now congratulate yourself on your strengths and strive to improve your weaknesses. Keep it simple!

THIS IS *YOUR* LIFE...IS IT SATISFYING?

Review the major areas of your life and note the important aspects of each area. Write down the *first* thing that comes to mind (spend no more than one minute on this) regarding each of the major aspects of your life. At the end of your sentence, rate each on a satisfaction scale from 0 - 10, ten being totally satisfied.

Examples:

Social : (Friends)   "I have several very good friends" 10 = { totally satisfied }
Health : (Exercise)   "I can't seem to find time."
0 = { dissatisfied }

I   **Personal:**

   a) parents_____

   b) mate_____

   c) children_____

   d) sex_____

   e) friends_____

Create Yourself...

II Work:

a) types of work - 1_____

  2_____

  3_____

b) physical aspect of your work -

_____

c) intellectual aspect of your work -

_____

d) emotional aspect of your work -

_____

III Health:

a) food _____

b) exercise _____

c) positive mental attitude_____

d) relaxation techniques _____

IV Social:

a) activities _____

b) hobbies _____

c) interests _____

d) family _____

e) friends _____

Now go back and record the *approach* you used in every aspect of each area, selecting from the following A, B, C, or D.

A - "I take action to *create* the situations I need and want."

B - "I choose according to my needs."

C - "I depend mostly on facts, statistics, and research for my choices."

D - "I usually count on other's opinions and values for my choices."

Examples:

Social : (Friends) "I have several very good friends." 10 - B = {choose according to needs.}

Look over your list carefully, and try changing any C or D approaches to A or B approaches in any area where you are less than totally satisfied.

Example :

Health : (Exercise) "I can't seem to find time."
0 - C {I depend } CHANGE TO *A { I take action }*

YOU AND YOUR PRIORITIES

If you really want to be in control, you must accept the fact that those habits may seem nice but that being in control is even nicer. You need to search down deep and ask yourself, "Is this my number one priority?" For example, is eating sinful foods more important to you than being permanently slim and healthy? And, is the fact that you lack time or are bored with exercise more important than reaching your health goals?

The Enemy Within!

(Answer Yes or No) Do you want to be healthy, emotionally and physically, and...

a) Enjoy sex _____

b) Have lots of energy to do more (therefore, no more excuses) _____

c) Enjoy good health (no more excuses not to do things) _____

State some additional reasons why someone might

41

subconsciously want to remain emotionally and/or physically unhealthy:

1. _____
2. _____
3. _____
4. _____
5. _____

Note: Are any of these priorities preventing you from reaching your goal?

Your Personal Priorities in Life:

It is **most** important to **me** to :

1. _____
2. _____
3. _____
4. _____
5. _____
6. _____
7. _____
8. _____
9. _____
10. _____

List ten reasons why you *want* to be healthy and positive, no matter what!

1._____
2._____
3._____
4._____
5._____
6._____
7._____
8._____
9._____
10._____

HALF-FULL OR HALF-EMPTY???

Become aware of your illogical stinkin' thinkin'! Unpleasant feelings, which lead to unwanted behaviors, indicate that you are thinking negatively about something and believing it to be true. Your emotions follow your thoughts just as surely as baby ducks follow their mother. (The *fact* that they are following her does not prove that she knows where she is going.) I rest my case.

"As a man thinketh in his heart, so is he," goes the famous quote - and not, "As a man feeleth in his heart, so is he." The former is true. You think, you feel, you are. If you think negative thoughts, you will *feel* negative about yourself and everything around you. This negative emotion will *feel* realistic and lend an aura of credibility to the illogical thought that created it. And the vicious circle begins.

Let's go back to the negative thought that created the negative feeling. Your thoughts are based upon your *attitude*. I ask you now, "Is the glass of water half-full or is it half-empty?" The negative thinker focuses on what is lacking while the positive thinker focuses on what is in the glass. Technically, both attitudes are correct. An attitude is a way of looking at something and determines how we shall approach a situation. A positive attitude says: "I can make a difference." As Ralph Waldo Emerson stated: "No matter how oppressive a situation, nothing can take away the fact that I can choose how I will respond." Realizing that you always have a choice in any situation gives you a sense of freedom and self-control which carries over to all aspects of your behavior and your life.

Examples of stinkin' thinkin' that lead to bad feelings that lead to more stinkin' thinkin':

Half-empty: "It's a rainy day and my whole vacation is ruined." (*Note - Even when the sun comes out, you'll still be grumbling about what might have been, and guess what, you will ruin your vacation.*)

Half-full: "Nonsense, I'll take this opportunity to make new friends in the exercise room, and when the weather clears,

I'll have plenty of time for outdoor activities. Who knows what possibilities await me?"

Can *you* come up with a creative opportunity for all of the situations below? Remember it's easy to think positive when things are great, but the truly positive thinker sees opportunities even in the darkest times.

1. A friend calls you at the last minute to cancel plans because of illness.

_____

_____

_____

_____

_____

2. You've planned a wonderful dinner for you and your mate - the phone rings and your mother keeps you on the line. Meanwhile, the steak is burnt to a crisp.

_____

_____

_____

_____

_____

3. You're stuck in traffic and late for an appointment.

_____

_____

_____

_____

_____

4. You decide to see a movie you've been *waiting* for. You arrive at the theatre and it is sold out.

_____

_____

_____

_____

_____

5. You're already late for an important social engagement. You put on your last clean pair of slacks and in your hurry, spill coffee all over yourself.

_____

_____

_____

_____

_____

6. You drive several miles out of your way for a sale item, then discover the store is sold out.

_____

_____

_____

_____

_____

7. You and a friend make plans to attend a special meeting. You get there and find that the meeting is postponed.

_____

_____

_____

_____

_____

8. You order a new large screen TV and invite a few friends over. The set is delivered but the picture is fuzzy and unclear.

_____

_____

_____

_____

_____

9. You're scheduled to depart for your dream vacation and the airline cancels the flight because of bad weather.

_____

_____

_____

_____

_____

10. It's your turn to carpool and the car doesn't start.

_____

_____

_____

_____

_____

Keep in mind that even if your only choice is to take a *seemingly* negative situation and turn it into an opportunity to learn from the experience, this choice makes the difference between ultimate defeat or success.

Here are ten positive statements that you can use daily to reinforce the attitude that even in the darkest times, there is *always* a creative opportunity just waiting to be discovered.

(Before you begin, take several deep, relaxing breaths and tell yourself, "I am calm and at peace from within.")

1. "No matter what happens, I am me."
2. "Opportunities are all around me, just waiting to be discovered."
3. "I am excited about the possibilities!"
4. "I believe in the sun, even when it isn't shining."
5. "I am free to choose to go forward."
6. "I am satisfied with all aspects of my life."

7. "I am wonderful!"

8. "I am healthy!"

9. "I am confident!"

10. *"I know I can do it!"*

Maintaining a positive attitude in adversities is the key to self-control. Rather than focusing on being the victim, (half-empty attitude), you are taking control of you *and* your habits. (Half-full attitude).

WHAT'S STOPPING YOU?

Let's find out what you need more of. Is it determination...or fortitude...or enthusiasm...or application...or tenacity...or faith? These are all components of your willpower and sometimes it's difficult to identify which ones need to be worked on. Strengthening one component actually has a beneficial effect on the others, so let's see if we can identify exactly what will help *you* become in control of you.

Have you ever made the following (or similar) statements? Answer Yes or No:

1. "I get started on a program, then after a while, I quit." _____

2. "When I see chocolate, (or a favorite food) I just can't resist." _____

3. "Sometimes my goals are just too much work." _____

4. "I don't have time to concentrate." _____

5. "Sometimes I quit because I just can't see myself succeeding." _____

6. "I don't mind working at this now but after a while it's too much for me." _____

7. "I can rationalize very easily, making excuses sound O.K." _____

8. "Sure, I want to gain confidence, but I don't know if I can." _____

9. "If my family makes fun of me, I give up." _____

10. "I want to reach my goal, but a few months more or less don't matter." _____

11. "If I see a commercial, I want what's being advertised." _____

12. "When I'm in a group, I seem to do whatever they do." _____

13. "I've tried lots of programs - I keep trying new ones that come out." _____

14. "It doesn't seem as though I'm improving."

    _____

15. "I usually lose weight, then gain it back, then try another diet." _____

16. "It's hard for me to exercise because I have arthritis." (Or whatever) _____

17. "I'll stick to healthy foods, but think about

forbidden ones." _____

18. "This is pretty important to me, I think I'll try."

_____

19. "I'll never make it, I have too far to go." _____

20. "If I neglect what I should do, I get disgusted and give up." _____

If you answered Yes to:	You need more:
1 - 8 - 13 - 15	Determination
2 - 7 - 12	Fortitude
3 - 10 - 18	Enthusiasm
4 - 11 - 17	Application
5 - 9 - 14 - 19	Faith
6 - 16 - 20	Tenacity

Now, get your willpower components in shape and you're sure to be a winner this time. Let's go for it!

DO I...DO I...OR DON'T I ???

Is your willpower letting you down? A strong desire, fanned by your imagination, equals willpower. Now isn't that simple? No need to fight with yourself - no need to constantly focus on what not to do - but aim instead for what you *want* to do. (Let's not be like the child who was asked by her mother, "Why are you unhappy? What do you want?" The child replied, "I don't know, I thought you knew and were going to give it to me.") This, therefore, is the real question: what do you *want* to do?

Before you answer that question ask yourself: Am I the captain of my ship? Check yes or no.

1. Can I resist a certain food or drink that I like but isn't good for me? _____

2. Am I normally on time for appointments?

   _____

3. Do I usually get up at the same time? _____

4. Can I interrupt a favorite TV Program and turn my attention to exercising? _____

5. Can I 'imagine' myself as confident and happy?

———

Take any NO responses and work on the corresponding situation until you have mastered it several times. If all of your answers were YES, you are the captain of your ship. *Ahoy!*

And now, what is it that you *really want* to do? Fill in all blank spaces below:

1. *I really want* to _____,
   therefore I shall begin by _____
   _____, *now.*

2. *I really want* to _____,
   therefore I shall begin by _____
   _____, *now.*

3. *I really want* to _____,
   therefore I shall begin by _____
   _____, *now.*

4. *I really want* to _____,
   therefore I shall begin by _____
   _____, *now.*

5. *I really want* to _____,

therefore I shall begin by _____

_____, *now.*

6. *I really want* to _____,

therefore I shall begin by _____

_____, *now.*

7. *I really want* to _____,

therefore I shall begin by _____

_____, *now.*

8. *I really want* to _____,

therefore I shall begin by _____

_____, *now.*

9. *I really want* to _____,

therefore I shall begin by _____

_____, *now.*

10. *I really want* to _____,

therefore I shall begin by _____

_____, *now.*

There. You've made your choices. You know
what you want and you have decided to begin now.
Forget about tomorrow and the next day and
concentrate only on right now. Tell yourself that
when tomorrow comes you'll make the right choices

but for now you need live only in the present moment!

Read the previous exercise aloud every day for the next ten days. Being in control of yourself is an on-going, moment-to-moment process. Remember that every moment holds the potential for total misery or total fulfillment. The choice is yours.

ARE YOU IN CONTROL OF YOU ???

Answer Yes or No :

1. When going out socially in a group, do you usually ask the others what they will wear?

   _____

2. Do you often avoid going anywhere by yourself?

   _____

3. Do you usually keep quiet during friendly debates? _____

4. If you and your friends were at a party, and they were eating foods you would normally avoid, would you join them? _____

5. Would you buy a newly advertised product even if you were satisfied with a similar product?

   _____

6. If you had an item of clothing that a friend had previously laughed at, would you avoid wearing it again while with this same person? _____

7. Do you vote according to the opinions of your friends? _____

8. If your best friend buys something new, do you

often buy something similar? _____

9. If someone in authority makes a statement, do
   you assume it to be correct? _____

10. Do you usually accept a dare? _____

Select the questions above to which you answered Yes
and complete the following:

If I were in control of myself and my life I would...

1. _____

2. _____

3. _____

4. _____

5. _____

6. _____

7. _____

8. _____

9. _____

10. _____

Now, choose at least two of your statements above
as you practice being in control of that particular
situation for the next seven days.

Next week, select two more of your statements and

practice those control exercises for at least seven days. Continue down the list until you have successfully practiced for at least one week all of the control questions. At this point you should be able to answer No to all of the original questions.

Note: If the opportunity for these situations doesn't present itself, create one in your mind and mentally practice being in control.

Isn't It Great To Be In Control Of You ?

Here's an exercise to help you overcome procrastination. As you become more in control of yourself and your life, you will also become more productive. Consequently, your degree of satisfaction will increase, raising your self-esteem as well.

Anti-procrastination Exercise: (use scale of 1 - 10)
   Example:
   1. Weed the garden
       How difficult did you anticipate this to be? __10__
       How difficult was it actually? __5__

1. _____

    How difficult did you anticipate this to be? ____

    How difficult was it actually? ____

2. _____

    How difficult did you anticipate this to be? ____

    How difficult was it actually? ____

3. _____

    How difficult did you anticipate this to be? ____

    How difficult was it actually? ____

4. _____

    How difficult did you anticipate this to be? ____

    How difficult was it actually? ____

5. _____

    How difficult did you anticipate this to be? ____

    How difficult was it actually? ____

6. _____

    How difficult did you anticipate this to be? ____

    How difficult was it actually? ____

7. _____

    How difficult did you anticipate this to be? ____

    How difficult was it actually? ____

8. _____

How difficult did you anticipate this to be? ____

How difficult was it actually? ____

9.   _____

How difficult did you anticipate this to be? ____

How difficult was it actually? ____

10. _____

How difficult did you anticipate this to be? ____

How difficult was it actually? ____

Note: If your activity requires a great deal of time, break it down into several tasks.

IS IT REALLY THAT DIFFICULT?

How difficult is it really, to think positive in all situations? Difficult you say? Perhaps you're blowing it up out of proportion. Or, maybe you're jumping to conclusions. If you didn't do this successfully in the past, does it mean you can't do it now? You're smarter and wiser and certainly more aware than you've ever been. Are you willing to try? If so, you're in for a delightful surprise. It's not half as difficult as you think it is. Let's try an experiment for one week.

Thinking Positive

Record the difficulty you *anticipated,* and the *actual* difficulty encountered while thinking positive. Also note your confidence level in this area.

Example:

	Anticipated Difficulty	Actual Difficulty	Confidence Level
Mon	_100%_	_40%_	_90%_

64

Create Yourself...

	Anticipated Difficulty	Actual Difficulty	Confidence Level
Mon	_____	_____	_____
Tues	_____	_____	_____
Wed	_____	_____	_____
Thurs	_____	_____	_____
Fri	_____	_____	_____
Sat	_____	_____	_____
Sun	_____	_____	_____

Go back and see how you wasted time and energy by *anticipating* much more difficulty than was actually experienced. Resolve not to waste any more energy by anticipating negatively.

Today can mark a real turning point for you... the rest of the way is easy.

THE WORLD'S GREATEST CON GAME

Are you perfect...or, are you human? Perfection is the ultimate illusion. There is no perfection. This is the world's greatest con game. It promises happiness and delivers disappointment. The more you expect to be perfect, the worse will be the disappointment because perfection is not reality. Then comes the steady decline of motivation in all areas because you begin to fear failure.

Perfect people? Where? Look around you. Look at a tree. You can always find ways to improve even the most perfectly formed tree if you look hard enough. A perfect lawn? Whoops! There's a brown spot, or a weed. You can always find ways to improve something, and that's terrific because it keeps us striving to get better and better. Perfect people? Look more closely. (Not on television because they camouflage the mistakes.) Look beyond the obvious and you'll find some imperfection, some room for improvement, everywhere.

Fear is the energy that fuels the compulsive behavior: fear of criticism, fear of failure, based upon lack of confidence. Ask yourself, "What is it that I am afraid of, what's the worse that could happen?" For example, what if you didn't do the exercise for the full amount of time. Does that mean you can never exercise the required time again? Does it mean you can never exercise again period? Of course not - this is exaggerated, false thinking that uses up precious time and energy. You did your best at that time and it's O.K.

Here are some representative samples of exaggerated, false thinking and the actual reality:

FALSE	REALITY
I am starving right now.	Nonsense, you ate just a few hours ago.
I was scared to death.	Think about this one... you're still here.

I never have time for anything.	Actually, you have time to do what you have chosen. For example, you have taken the time to read this right now.
Nobody loves me.	*Somebody* loves you - your mother, a friend, your pet, etc...
As a child, I was never happy.	Never? Think again - find some tiny memory, some bit of pleasure, a ride on a swing, a favorite toy...
The exercise is too much for me.	Nonsense. You can start very gradually, *patiently* working your way up to your desired level. The trick is to simply **BEGIN NOW!!!**

I have no willpower.   Everyone has willpower.
                            You've used it
                            successfully in the past...
                            when you graduated from
                            kindergarden, or got a
                            college degree, or found a
                            mate, or got a job, or
                            crossed the street.

Using these examples as a guide, insert your own
favorite false statement on the left side. On the right
side, write down the actual reality.

_____ _____

_____ _____

_____ _____

_____ _____

_____ _____

_____ _____

_____ _____

_____ _____

_____ _____

_____ _____

_____   _____

_____   _____

_____   _____

_____   _____

_____   _____

_____   _____

_____   _____

_____   _____

_____   _____

_____   _____

_____   _____

_____   _____

_____   _____

_____   _____

_____   _____

_____   _____

_____   _____

_____   _____

_____   _____

_____   _____

_____   _____

IF YOU GOOF UP...IT'S O.K.

Admit that you are not perfect and that you can make mistakes. Mistakes ultimately work in our favor; they help us to try harder, to learn faster. You're learning when you make mistakes, so what's the problem? If you fear making mistakes, you'll procrastinate and become afraid to attempt anything. You may as well admit that you are human and will make your share of mistakes, just like everyone else. Dare to be human! You'll be so much more satisfied with yourself and your life.

I repeat, *accept* the fact that you are human, and therefore not perfect. You have a choice. You can choose to be perfect and end up in misery, setting yourself up for unrealistic expectations; if you make a mistake you'll feel shame and put yourself down. Or, you can choose to be human, do your very best, and feel great about whatever you do, thereby enhancing your self-esteem.

Let's use simple logic for a moment. Human beings make mistakes. Agreed? You are a human

71

being, right? Therefore, it is a logical conclusion that you will make mistakes because you are human, and not because you are stupid.

We all learn from our mistakes. Madame Curie discovered radium after hundreds of mistakes...as a child learning to walk you fell down, and you picked yourself up. And you did this over and over again until you got it right. Were you stupid or were you human? Mistakes promote growth and force you to practice, to try, to get creative in order to get it right. What an opportunity! Would you really want to be perfect? That would mean no room for improvement. How boring. You would know all the answers - somewhat like being in the first grade all of your life. You'd probably have excellent marks but no opportunity to grow.

Write down 10 so-called mistakes you've made in the past and force yourself to find some good that came out of it.

Example:

  1. A bad marriage - a wonderful child

72

1._____

2._____

3._____

4._____

5._____

6._____

7._____

8._____

9._____

10._____

And now you are learning to forget about your mistakes and focus on your successes. Tell yourself, "If I goof up, it's O.K. - I'm human. I'll start right over again. I'm beginning today. *NOW!!!* "

HOWEVER...

We've said it's O.K. to make mistakes, it's O.K. to goof up if we learn as we go along, we've also said not to expect to be perfect - but, nowhere have we said you don't have to commit to doing your very best. "I'll try," you say. "Maybe." Think about what you are saying. This is cheap talk that can only lead to an all expense paid guilt trip.

Saying, "I'll try," as opposed to "I can," is semantic double-talk. Your conscious mind says: "Of course I want to be in control," while your subconcious is saying, "I'm not sure I want to give up my old habits yet. Maybe I'm not ready to get out of this comfortable rut. I'll go along for now and let you know when I'm sick of trying." Sick of trying usually happens when the stress of life weakens your determination to succeed. Enter excusitis! "I had to go to a party and you know the kinds of food they serve," or - "I have such a busy schedule today, I'll exercise tomorrow." Excuses straight from your subconscious! Don't listen. No excuses = no guilt

74

later on which would lead to more problems. Simply make the *decision* to commit now. No questions, no wondering about how you'll do it; let your desire to become confident, healthy, and attractive be the fire that fuels your *decision* to succeed and commit, and in that order. The 'hows' will automatically follow.

Make the following no-excuse commitments, week-by-week, and begin *NOW!*

Example: I make the no-excuse commitment to

    __exercise every day_____, and I begin now!

Week #1: I make the no-excuse commitment to

_____, and I begin now!

Week #2: I make the no-excuse commitment to

_____, and I begin now!

Week #3: I make the no-excuse commitment to

_____, and I begin now!

Week #4: I make the no-excuse commitment to

_____, and I begin now!

Week #5: I make the no-excuse commitment to

_____, and I begin now!

Week #6: I make the no-excuse commitment to

_____, and I begin now!

Week #7: I make the no-excuse commitment to

_____, and I begin now!

Note: When you've completed the seven weeks of commitments, you will become 'aware' of a new self-respect and belief in yourself.

YOU CAN DO IT!

LET GO OF WHAT'S EATING YOU!

What you feel on the inside reflects on the outside.
You have learned that emotions and/or feelings follow
thoughts and that you have the power to reject all
thoughts that may disturb you. Let me tell you that
forgiveness of others, and yourself, is absolutely
essential to your inner peace and good health.
Forgiveness will release your grip on negative
emotions such as: anger, hurt, guilt, fear, resentment,
etc..., making it possible to start fresh in *seemingly*
unrelated areas of your life. It's all relative.

Speaking of relatives, let's begin at the beginning,
with Mom and Dad, the rest of the family, and move
on from there. Very often we are more impatient and
judgemental with close family members than with
anyone else in the world because our relatives never
seem to live up to our expectations, or perhaps we feel
they mistreated us long ago.

Many of us carry this emotional garbage, (which
somehow seems to wind up in our mouths) not only
towards family members but also toward our loved

ones. Too many love relationships are overcrowded
with garbage from past relationships. Some people
carry garbage such as: hurt, resentment, guilt, fear,
anger, and others, for years and years, without
realizing that the weight of the garbage is weighing
them down, holding them back, perhaps keeping them
in a constant state of physical and/or emotional
disrepair. Certainly, none of us want to be held back
by the unfortunate things that happened to us in the
past.

It is possible to let go and get rid of (and in that
order) the garbage! Ask yourself why you seem to be
walking on eggshells around this person who is in
your life? Very often, we get into the habit of being
anxious around this person because we're afraid of
either hurting them or being hurt by them.
Consequently, we tend to overreact to every little
thing they say or do; or, we worry about our every
action being misinterpreted. As a result, emotional
distance sets in and pretty soon we feel uncomfortable
with this person we care so deeply about. Whether
this is a parent, child, sibling, spouse, or friend, that
emotional distance is garbage and physically and/or

emotionally damaging to you.

We need to ask ourselves,"Is there something for which I need to forgive this person?" Or, "Is there something I need to forgive myself for that relates to this person?" Many times, a basic need to forgive starts with our parents. So they didn't live up to our expectations of what a 'perfect' parent should be - *so what?* They're human, remember? Are we so perfect? Look at their parents if you want to understand your parents - and forgive them, love them, not for their sake, but for your sake - for your own physical and/or emotional well-being.

One way to begin is to write out a list of hurts and resentments toward anyone and everyone who has hurt or mistreated you. When finished, read it over and be sure you haven't forgotten anything, then - burn it, knowing that if you do you are letting go of all the hurt and the anger contained in the letter.

If someone consistently makes you feel guilty, here's a little trick you can use. Write down ZINGER #1, #2, #3, #4, etc...thinking up your own ZINGERS. Then read the statement below your ZINGER: "Cancel that, because I am wonderful!"

Create Yourself...

Examples:

ZINGER : *"Did you get a job yet?"*

"Cancel that, because I am wonderful!"

ZINGER : *"When are you going to get married?"*

"Cancel that, because I am wonderful!"

ZINGER #1:_____

"Cancel that, because *I am wonderful!*"

ZINGER #2:_____

"Cancel that, because *I am wonderful!*"

ZINGER #3:_____

"Cancel that, because *I am wonderful!*"

ZINGER #4:_____

"Cancel that, because *I am wonderful!*"

ZINGER #5:_____

"Cancel that, because *I am wonderful!*"

ZINGER #6:_____

"Cancel that, because *I am wonderful!*"

ZINGER #7:_____

"Cancel that, because *I am wonderful!*"

ZINGER #8:_____

"Cancel that, because *I am wonderful!*"

ZINGER #9:_____

"Cancel that, because *I am wonderful!*"

Create Yourself...

ZINGER #10:_____

"Cancel that, because *I am wonderful!*"

Now when you actually visit or call your guilt -
inducing friend or relative and you hear the familiar
remark, you can take a deep breath and laugh to
yourself with a sense of humor saying: "There it is -
good old ZINGER #4... cancel that because *I am
wonderful!*"

Notice that it's much easier to stand up for yourself
and not feel guilty when *you* have a sense of control
over the situation.

If you've been arguing with a loved one or a
relative for some time, you can break the pattern by
focusing on - "three things I appreciate about you."
Too often, we only find fault with those we care
about, forgetting what we like about those people in
our lives. Again, the best place to start is with our
parents, describing three things we appreciate about
them. Simply say to them: "Let's try something - let's
each tell ourselves three things we appreciate about
each other, I'll go first." If they don't cooperate, do it
anyway and say, "That's O.K. - whenever you're

ready."

I have witnessed several people doing this exercise. At first they are reluctant because this is so different from the usual sarcasm and complaining that characterizes the way they speak to each other. When they finally go ahead and describe three things they appreciate about the other, there is first an element of surprise. These are usually things that they've never heard before from this person and the exercise ends with hugs and tears.

I am not suggesting that you place yourself in unreasonable situations - I am simply saying that you need to forgive in your heart. But, you may answer, "I have the right to be angry, or hurt, or whatever." Of course you do. Anger is legally permitted in this country, as are the other negative emotions. The point is - is it to *your* advantage to remain angry? Will anyone really benefit from this? On the other hand, the person who will be hurt the most is you.

There is an old legend about a man who was arrested and then taken down a long stairway into a dark dungeon by a ferocious-looking jailer who carried a very large key. He put his prisoner in the cell and shut the door with a bang. Every day the jailer would bring the man bread and water, then shut the door of the cell. Finally, after twenty years, the prisoner decided he could no longer stand being locked up in prison. His solution...suicide. He came up with a plan that included attacking the jailer when he brought the bread and water, concluding that the jailer would kill him in self-defense. Carefully preparing for the event, the prisoner examined the cell door and accidentally turned the handle - the door opened! He walked out a free man realizing that all those years he had been a prisoner in belief only.

Like the prisoner in the dungeon, the choice is yours and you can opt to be free.

You And Your Enemies - Past Or Present - Living Or Dead

Write down the names of persons whom you feel have hurt you deeply:

1._____

2._____

3._____

4._____

5._____

6._____

7._____

8._____

9._____

10._____

Repeat the following exercise for each person listed above, one at a time. Do this daily for 21 days. Make yourself comfortable, close your eyes, and take several, deep, relaxing breaths. Now, imagine that you are sitting in a darkened theatre, third row center, very relaxed and totally at peace. The curtain rises, and the spotlight is on the person above. Visualize good things happening to this person, things that you know to be meaningful for them. Imagine them smiling and happy. Hold this image for a few moments, then let it fade away.

After twenty one days of doing the previous exercise, find as many good qualities about these

Create Yourself...

persons as you can, and list below:

NAME	QUALITIES
1._____	_____
	_____
2._____	_____
	_____
3._____	_____
	_____
4._____	_____
	_____
5._____	_____
	_____
6._____	_____
	_____
7._____	_____
	_____
8._____	_____
	_____
9._____	_____
	_____
10._____	_____
	_____

NOTE: If you get stuck on any one person, you need to work on this some more. Place this person on the stage and keep looking for something positive about them until you find it.

It's never too late to let go of emotional garbage and make a fresh start, at least from your perspective.

SO WHAT???

Is it really so terrible if someone disapproves of you? Sometimes, friends and family make it difficult for us to be positive about life and its challenges. Perhaps they, caught in a comfortable rut, disapprove of you being emotionally in control - taking on the challenges of life with complete confidence, using the tools that I give you, that I use myself, daily.

Why does disapproval pose such a threat to you? Maybe your thinking goes somewhat like this: "If one person disapproves of me, it means that everyone could disapprove of me. That might mean something is wrong with me." If this line of thinking applies to you, it follows that your moods will shoot up every time you are being stroked. This is illogical because you are overlooking the fact that it is only *your* thoughts and beliefs which have the power to elevate your spirits. It must come from within! Another's approval has no power to affect your mood unless you *believe* what they say is valid. If you believe, however, that a compliment is earned, it is this *belief* that makes you feel good. Before you can experience mood elevation you must validate external approval and this validation represents your personal self-approval.

For example: Suppose you walked into a nursing home and an elderly, confused patient said to you, "You are my savior...let me kiss your hand - you are wonderful!" Would this extreme approval elevate your mood? Probably not. Most people would feel nervous and uncomfortable at this outburst. Why? Because you don't believe that what this person is saying is valid, therefore you discredit the comments.

Only *your* beliefs about yourself can affect the way you feel. Others may say what they will about you, good or bad, but only *your* thoughts will influence your emotions. If you rely on the opinions of others, the moment someone expresses criticism you will crash emotionally, allowing these people to manipulate you. At this point, you may give in to their 'negativity', give up your positive attitude, for fear of being rejected. This is where you set yourself up for emotional blackmail!

Let's imagine that you make a second trip to the

nursing home. This time another confused patient approaches you and says, "You are wearing a black coat, this means you are evil." Would you feel depressed because of this disapproval? Why not? Because you don't believe this person's statement to be true. Hence, did it ever occur to you that if someone disapproves of you, it is more than likely, *their* problem, period.

Naturally, there are those times when disapproval results from an actual error on your part. SO WHAT? Does this indicate that you are a totally worthless person? Of course not - we are imperfect human beings, needing to make mistakes so as to learn - to grow. Remember that another's negative reaction can only be directed at a specific thing you do - not at your worth as a person. You're deeply mistaken if you think that outside approval and/or disapproval are the proper gauges with which to measure your self-worth.

Have you ever snapped at someone when you were tired or upset? Have you ever expressed disapproval toward someone? We've all, at one time or another, done these things...but ask yourself if you were making a judgement as to this person's worth? Did you, while criticizing, determine that this person was a totally worthless human being? Do *you* have the power to make such a determination about anyone? And, do *they* have the power to make such a determination about you? Haven't you ever, in the heat of anger, said to someone, "You're no good!" Once you cool off, don't you think this was a bit exaggerated? If you can understand that your disapproval does not have the power to lower the worth of another person, then you can also understand that *they* have no power to lower your worth, unless you allow it to happen - unless you believe it to be true. Is it realistic to make yourself miserable and unhappy just because someone else has a problem that day, or even every day? Keep in mind that it's *their* problem!

"But," you say, "I was raised this way; as a small child I was always put down and criticized." Granted that as a child you were not mature enough to realize that Mommy and Daddy were tired or irritable, for reasons that may have had absolutely nothing to do with you. Or, perhaps they simply didn't know better, and did the best they knew how, at that time. Maybe you *assumed* that everything they told you was true, so if they said, "You can't do that," you literally believed it to be true.

I am reminded of the little girl who, at the age of seven, overheard her mother and grandmother talking in the bedroom. The child's father had died and the mother said, "Now I have nobody and nothing to live for!" The little girl never let on that she had heard this conversation and simply assumed that she wasn't worth anything. As she grew up she became more and more rebellious towards her mother, but never quite understood why.

Let's look at this situation as adults. It's obvious that the child overreacted, that the mother's comments were laced with the bitterness of the loss that she felt at the time. Her words had *nothing* to do with her child, but only with her despair of the situation.

If you've picked up the bad habit of *automatically* looking down on yourself every time someone disapproves of you, isn't it time - as an adult - to think this through realistically and outgrow this habit? *LET IT GO!*

"But," you may ask, "If this is an *automatic*

reaction or response, how can I stop it?" Or - "If this is learned behavior, what can I do about it?"

Simple. You can choose to *interrupt* this automatic response with an act ot will - an interrupting behavior. Read on...

INTERRUPT OLD BEHAVIOR PATTERNS

Does this sound familiar? Do you automatically crave and/or reach for something when:

a) someone treats you unfairly

b) someone expects you to do something you'd rather not do

c) someone interrupts as you are doing something important to you

Write down 10 examples of situations and/or conditions to which you automatically react.

Examples:

a) a favorite TV program _____

b) your mother (or whomever) calls you _____

1. _____

2. _____

3. _____

4. _____

5. _____

6._____

7._____

8._____

9._____

10._____

Note: how many of these occur more frequently that others.

Choose to interrupt the automatic reaction with an act of will, (interrupting behavior) thereby inserting a behavior between the stimulus (situation) and the automatic response. You may or may not decide to act in a more loving way to yourself as well as others, but whatever your decision, at least you are in control of your behavior as opposed to your behavior being in control of you and your habits.

Interrupting Behavior: From now on, whenever any of the above stimuli occur, you will rub your thumb and your forefinger together, five times, as a gentle reminder that *you* are in control of your behavior and not your behavior in control of you.

Create Yourself...

Example:

Stimulus = My mother called and criticized me.

Automatic Response = food, alcohol, cigarette, etc.

OR

Stimulus = My mother called and criticized me.

Interrupting Behavior = rub thumb and forefinger 5

times

Controlled Response = I relaxed and politely

changed the subject.

After using interruptive behavior, note how you responded to the situation and/or condition.

Situation	Response
1._____	_____
2._____	_____
3._____	_____
4._____	_____
5._____	_____
6._____	_____
7._____	_____
8._____	_____

9._____ _____

10._____ _____

MASTER THE CLOCK!

How would you like to manage and organize your time? How would you like to have more time? Never happen, you say? We'll see. About 75% of people who are stressed out tell me that they lack time for exercise and positive conditioning. They run around in circles with no time for exercise, meditation, or positive statements. Time is the #1 excuse. Let's begin, therefore, by putting *you* in control of your time.

You can clear clutter, watch television, and create time all at once by combining and selecting activities. Everyone needs a desk, some file folders, a wastebasket, and an answering machine. Mail, bills, and periodicals, can be sorted out daily while watching your favorite TV program. Set yourself up with a letter opener, a wastepaper basket, and some file folders labeled bills due...bills paid...to read...etc... Decide which program you want to watch as you turn this so-called wasted time into productive time. Even better yet, tape your favorite show and do this when *you* think it's a good time. *Note: Resolve to watch only those programs you choose. As you organize the paperwork, first in your mind, then in reality, you begin to open up blocks of time for the more satisfying, important things in your life, such as good nutrition, physical exercise, and positive conditioning.*

List ten things you can do while watching your favorite television program:

1._____
2._____
3._____
4._____
5._____
6._____
7._____
8._____
9._____
10._____

The satisfaction that you derive from this both enjoyable and productive time will keep you away from negative habits and even more important, give you that feeling of accomplishment and self-control.

TV and Telephone = Time

Time, one of our most precious commodities, can
be created by:

1. Combining tasks with your favorite TV programs
2. Determining when you will make or return
   telephone calls

Since we've already discussed the combination of
tasks or hobbies with well-chosen television programs,
let's move on to that *number one time waster*, the
telephone. Do you literally jump when the phone
rings? Do you realize how this instrument, and
whoever is on the other end, has control of your
precious time? Is responding to this call more
important than your health, emotional or otherwise?

Record, for one week, the amount of telephone calls
received, from whom, and the amount of time spent on
each call.

 # Calls Received

Mon _____

99

Create Yourself...

Tues   _____

Wed   _____

Thurs   _____

Fri   _____

Sat   _____

Sun   _____

Total calls:_____

From Whom

Mon   _____

Tues   _____

Wed   _____

Thurs   _____

Fri   _____

Sat   _____

Sun   _____

Time Spent

Mon   _____

Tues   _____

Wed   _____

Thurs _____

Fri _____

Sat _____

Sun _____

Total Time:_____

Add the amount of time spent on the telephone and ask yourself if you *choose* to spend your time in this way? Can you think of things you'd rather do with this block of time?

List at least ten things you would love to find time for:

1._____

2._____

3._____

4._____

5._____

6._____

7._____

8._____

9._____

10._____

Now, go back and check those calls which could have been *condensed* into one or two calls per week. You may be thinking, "How am I supposed to convince those people to call only once or twice weekly?" That's easy!

Always use an answering machine. The monitor will tell you if it's an emergency. This way, not only are *you* deciding when to return a call, which once again gives you a feeling of self-control, but *you* can condense those frequent calls to once or twice weekly. You can even use a speaker phone and combine your tasks. You are opening up blocks of time you never knew you had, all contributing to the realization of your goals.

Stop and Do Nothing

There are times when you simply want to do nothing. Therefore, you half-heartedly keep on going with mundane tasks, feeling frustrated and unhappy, (not to mention guilt) because you are procrastinating in doing the very things that would give you a sense of accomplishment. Now, the merry-go-round starts and the big question is how to get off. The longer you procrastinate, the worse you feel, and the worse you feel, the longer you procrastinate. Here's how to stop that merry-go-round and get off. The next time you feel like procrastinating, *stop and do nothing.* No need to feel guilty. Simply sit down and do absolutely nothing. No TV, no book, no telephone, no snack, no cigarette, *nothing.* Sit there for as long as it takes for you to get bored. Next, decide what you want to do NOW! Not tomorrow, or next week, but ask yourself, "How can I begin right now?" If you fail to come up with an answer, you need to sit and do nothing a little longer. When you do come up with an answer, say to yourself, "To begin is half-done," several times. Don't concern yourself with completing the task, just begin. You'll be amazed at how this works - every time.

Go With The Flow...

Any well-balanced, self-management system must include those 'unexpected' happenings that are a necessary part of our lives. Don't struggle...go with the flow of these happenings. Relax, remain flexible, and enjoy your ability to be free and in control.

SATISFYING ACTIVITIES...AND I DON'T MEAN WATCHING TV

Have you ever dreamed of pursuing a hobby or avocation? Have you been putting it off because of insufficient time or lack of confidence? Why not develop a relationship with yourself? Deliberately look for activities that you can do alone. Do you really need someone with you to enjoy flowers, or listen to good music, or enroll in a creative dance class, or amateur acting group, or whatever? Learn to savor enjoyment by yourself, as well as with others. Although friends are great, you needn't feel miserable when alone. You'll be pleasantly surprised to discover that you really can make it on your own, in all areas of your life.

Treat yourself with kindness and with love - as you would a friend. Tolerate your liabilities, use them as a 'signal', an opportunity, to practice the skills I teach you. Cancel any negative thoughts about yourself and appreciate your assets, thereby enhancing your confidence in your ability to succeed. If you think you can, you will!

Learning how to blend right brain activities into your daily life will complete your behavior modification program for permanent peace of mind and personal growth. Maybe you doubt that you have both left brain and right brain abilities. To check on your left brain, simply ask yourself if you can understand a language. If so, the left side of your brain is already using its skills of logic, analysis, and sequence. To check on your right brain, ask yourself if you have ever day-dreamed, or let your imagination go while walking along a beautiful beach, or felt really moved by a favorite song.

Generally speaking, the left side of your brain deals with language, numbers, logic, analysis, and sequencing. When this side of your brain is active, the right side goes into a relaxed, semi-meditative state. Similarly, when the right brain is active, the left side goes into the same relaxed, semi-meditative state.

The right brain, when active, deals with rhythm and music, color, imagination, day-dreaming, and spatial awareness. It is important not to think of yourself as unskilled in any of the areas. It is more accurate to realize that you have *developed* certain areas of your potential abilities while others may be dormant, for now. You can choose to awaken any dormant area that would satisfy you, regardless of age, simply by beginning, in some small way, the process through some type of related activity.

Studies have shown that the great geniuses of history were not unbalanced, right or left brain dominant people, but that they had a wide range of interests and activities. Some of the scientist day-dreamed during research, while the artists were, at times, analytical. Einstein devised imaginative games which he applied to physics. For example, he laid the foundation for his theory of relativity while imagining himself riding through the universe on a sunbeam. Each of us *needs* this balance between left and right brain activities and in any self-development program it is essential to see to it that both sides of your brain are actively balanced.

Assume that you have 100% of your time to devote to your satisfying activities. List your satisfying activities and record how much time you would *ideally* like to devote to each activity.

Create Yourself...

Satisfying Activities	Ideal % of time Devoted
1._____	_____
2._____	_____
3._____	_____
4._____	_____
5._____	_____
6._____	_____
7._____	_____
8._____	_____
9._____	_____
10._____	_____

Now, record the amount of time you *actually* spend on your satisfying actyivities.

Satisfying Acivities	Actual % of time Devoted
1._____	_____
2._____	_____
3._____	_____
4._____	_____
5._____	_____
6._____	_____
7._____	_____

Create Yourself...

8._____   _____

9._____   _____

10._____   _____

And finally, compare your ideal percentage with your actual percentage, and note the difference.

Example :

Activity	Ideal%	Actual %	Difference
1. Art	40%	2%	38%

Activity	Ideal%	Actual%	Difference
1._____	_____	_____	_____
2._____	_____	_____	_____
3._____	_____	_____	_____
4._____	_____	_____	_____
5._____	_____	_____	_____
6._____	_____	_____	_____
7._____	_____	_____	_____
8._____	_____	_____	_____
9._____	_____	_____	_____
10._____	_____	_____	_____

Examine the differences between your ideal life and your actual life. Whether or not you reach the 'ideal' is unimportant; the idea is to *begin* changing patterns so as to bring the 'ideal' and the 'actual' time devoted closer together, constantly zeroing in on your desired target. Your brain will then automatically begin its own self-correcting program.

Remember that it's not only O.K. to enjoy yourself, it's absolutely necessary! This is *your* life... do as you wish at least some of the time. Have fun!

WHAT TURNS YOU ON ???

You need to counterbalance your physical and intellectual activities with those that provide enjoyment, otherwise you may set in motion the same stress that preceded unwanted negative behaviors such as, fatigue, lack of motivation, etc... As you search to satisfy your own personal needs, keep in mind that the essential quality is *balance*. A *balanced* combination of physical, emotional, and intellectual objectives that give you fulfillment. Ask yourself if you may have neglected one of these areas in the past? Fine tune your general pursuits until they become clear and concise. Write objectives that focus on your behavior, and not the behavior of others.

What are some of life's pleasures that turn you on? Think about what you enjoyed as a child. An early morning walk in the woods on a summer day, with the birds singing their symphony all around you - reading a good book at the end of a snowy, winter day, wrapped in a cozy afghan, with a pot of homemade soup simmering on the stove nearby. These satisfy your emotional needs, while taking an interesting course at a local college would satisfy your intellectual needs. It's important to include these seemingly insignificant activities in your balanced program.

Write down 5 activities that you feel would satisfy your emotional needs.

Example:

Listening to your favorite music.

1._____

2._____

3._____

4._____

5._____

Write down 5 activities that you feel would satisfy your intellectual needs.

Example:

Watching an educational program on TV.

1._____

2._____

3._____

4._____

5._____

Write down 5 activities that you feel would satisfy your physical needs.

Example:

   Going for a brisk walk.

   Planning a delicious, low-calorie, nutritional meal just for you.

1._____

2._____

3._____

4._____

5._____

Become sensitive to your needs. Develop a deep sense of much-needed satisfaction in all areas of your life so as to achieve that peace and tranquility from within. Key word: BALANCE

Let's Define Your Gaols...

Ask yourself, "What goals do I want to reach in my lifetime?...In three to five years?...In the next year?"

Create Yourself...

Find a goal which fulfills a part of your life that you have disregarded in the past; list specific actions for each goal.

"What goals do I want to reach in my lifetime?"

1._____

   Specific actions: a) _____

                        b) _____

                        c) _____

2._____

   Specific actions: a) _____

                        b) _____

                        c) _____

3._____

   Specific actions: a) _____

                        b) _____

                        c) _____

"What goals do I want to reach in the next 3-5 years?"

1._____

   Specific actions: a) _____

                        b) _____

                        c) _____

2._____

Specific actions: a) _____

                  b) _____

                  c) _____

3._____

Specific actions: a) _____

                  b) _____

                  c) _____

"What goals do I want to reach in the next year?"

1._____

Specific actions: a) _____

                  b) _____

                  c) _____

2._____

Specific actions: a) _____

                  b) _____

                  c) _____

3._____

Specific actions: a) _____

                  b) _____

                  c) _____

Get excited about reaching your goals! Begin with the actions for meeting your short-term goals. Each success, however small, is a step closer to the top, which are your lifetime goals. If you stumble or fall along the way, pick yourself up and keep on goin'... See you at the top!!!

WHAT ARE YOU WORTH?

Let's take an inventory of your assets - let's put a dollar value on those that you possess right now. Fill in the dollar amounts and look this over often to remind yourself of your *real* worth.

Write down the dollar value of your good health - what is it worth to you? One million? Ten million? $_____

What is the good health of your mate, your friend, or your child worth to you? $_____

Add to this any other people whose good health you value. What is it worth to you? $_____

Now, what is your freedom as an American worth to you? $_____

What are your hands and feet worth to you? $_____

How about your eyes - what are they worth to you?

$_____

What about your mind? How much do you value it?
What price would you take? What is it worth?

$_____

Add all of this up to determine your net worth.
Today I am worth $_____

This can be a day of transition for you as you focus on your assets and forget about your lacks.

Let your self-esteem soar along with your assets!
You are already one of the wealthiest people on earth.

P M A... POSITIVE MENTAL ATTITUDE

How do you live a positive lifestyle on a daily basis? Positive living is as much a philosophy as it is a positive approach to life. The following are suggested guidelines that have proven helpful to thousands.

Meditate daily, taking a few minutes to reach your inner mind, while calm and at peace. Then, make positive statements about your conscious life activities. Dedicate each day, whether great or difficult, upon awakening and upon retiring as you say to yourself, "I am filled with positive energy, I am healthy, confident, and satisfied." Do this ten times in the morning and ten times in the evening in addition to your other conditioning statements.

Nullify negative thoughts the minute they surface into your mind. Negative vibrations destroy the physical health of your body, while at the same time, send out negative energy rays to others. Don't build an aura of negative vibrations around yourself by

118

allowing negative thought energies to accumulate in and around your mental atmosphere. Nullify negative spoken words. Thinking a negative thought is bad enough, but even worse if it slips out with the spoken words. If something negative does slip out, take a moment to nullify what you said, either out loud or in your own mind, saying 'cancel' immediately. After saying 'cancel', *replace* that negative thought with a positive statement such as: "I am filled with Positive Energy!"

Examples:

"Forget it. I can't do this. I can't stick to anything."

"Cancel - Cancel - Cancel - I can do anything I choose to do."

"I'm always so tired..."
"Cancel - I feel great!"

"I'm used to being poor. I never have any money."
"Cancel - I am becoming more and more

119

prosperous, everyday. "

I think you get the idea. *Think* about what you say.
Hear what you are saying. And, keep it *POSITIVE!*

Give thanks daily for all that comes to you from
your own inner source. Keep peace with yourself by
allowing the positive flow of energy within you to
flow freely, without restriction. Learn to go with the
flow...think positively by cultivating the type of mind
that can see good even in the darkest of temporary
conditions. Living in a temple of positive thoughts is
like setting up a beautiful home that draws wonderful
things to you.

Your positive thoughts are the diamonds, the
emeralds, and the rubies in the crown of your
kingdom.

P M A   PLUS...IMAGINATION

There can be no rainbow until the storm has passed. Remembering this will give you the courage to face the stress and the challenges of daily living. Just remember and imagine this for a moment: the deep voice of the thunder rumbling in the sky, then - a moment of stillness; the waiting rains as they pour down to the trembling earth until our world is washed and purified. Again remember and imagine the storm subsiding and finally, a beautiful rainbow as it appears on the horizon, resting lightly on the distant hills.

If you can remember and imagine all of this, then you surely know that storms come and go - that twilight is neither the end of the day nor the beginning - that time is but a circle, with no beginning and no ending, and that it is neither the coming nor the going that is of importance. What is important is the growth and the awareness and the beauty that one gathers in this interlude called life.

How very wise are those who choose to look
neither backward into the past, nor forward into the
future, but are aware of the possibilities that exist right
now, believing they can reach their goals, regardless
of past experiences, with a positive mental attitude.

Let's consider people who have been confronted
with a major trama or disaster in life. I'm talking
about being held prisoner of war, or being taken
hostage by terrorists, or getting lost on a frozen
mountaintop, or having one's home destroyed by a
flood or a fire, or losing a loved one. It's never quite
the same afterward. It's as if they lose something on
the inside as a result of the ordeal. Social scientists
have studied these people and discovered that while
some are destroyed by the experience, others survive
and rebuild their lives on an emotional level. What
seems to make a difference is the *attitude* that was
adopted during the ordeal. Those who did not survive
fell victim to an attitude of helplessness - that's
understandable - control over their lives was taken
away and there was little they could do about it.
Thus, the negative side of this became imprinted on

their mind. Those who did survive managed to adopt a different attitude. They fought the temptation to give up and looked for some way to regain some small bit of control. Even being able to make any *small* decision about their situation made a difference in their outlook. They searched hard to find the bright side, believing in the sun even when it wasn't shining.

The psychology of survivors proves that our mental attitude can have a definite effect on how we deal with challenges. It can make the difference between being victimized by problems or learning from them how to evolve and grow, and of course, how to attain our goals.

Suppose I were to ask you to assume that believing is everything - that your mind creates the world you live in, and - the body you live in, that you can actually *design* the way you want to look and feel because your mind can be trained to do this. Assuming that this is true, (and I can assure you that it is) wouldn't it be important not to dismiss it? What I am saying is STOP ANALYZING - take this

123

information and use it, practice it, enjoy it!

The magic formula is: take a positive mental attitude, add belief and imagination. This is a powerful combination. The imagination is, in fact, the way to direct the positive energy of belief and attitude, the belief and attitude that *you* can be happy and healthy by using your imagination. From imagination came the airplane, the light bulb, spacecraft, and Disney World - to name a few. Just think what could come from *your* imagination if you but stimulate it with positive ideas, positive 'pictures'.

To demonstrate how you can expand the power of your mind through imagery and imagination, let's try an experiment. Just sit back and close your eyes as you keep repeating to yourself that your mouth is becoming moist - your mouth is watering - is becoming juicy. Let yourself feel your mouth forming saliva.

Now relax and imagine a lemon. In your mind's eye see it's yellow skin; imagine cutting the lemon in half with a knife. Imagine that you are picking up one of the lemon halves, squeezing it to make beads of juice form on the surface. Imagine that you are bringing the lemon up to your mouth as you begin to suck on the juice. Notice how sharp and tangy lemon juice can be...it makes you pucker - notice how much your mouth is watering now.

Note: A slight pause as this author swallows.

You have just succeeded in using your mind and your imagination to create a physical reality. Can you see the limitless possibilities? Can you 'imagine' yourself as happy and healthy? This is the secret of imagery, of visualization - the response is automatic.

So again, it's your choice. You can reject what has already been proven to work, or - you can accept it and use it. You are free to choose. You can choose to be the victim or the WINNER! You can choose to turn your negatives into positives. You can choose to be content!

USING MENTAL IMAGERY

Wouldn't it be great if you didn't know who you were? Just think about this for a minute. If you didn't have a pre-conceived image of yourself, you could start fresh and create a NEW you! You wouldn't have the fears and the limitations of the old you. Maybe then the statement that you can be anything you want to be would be true for you. True, the new you might come across *new* fears and limitations along the way... but, when you had gone as far as you could with the new you, you could create a *newer* you. And, the things you can't do now you might do then...habits you have now, you might not have then...things that you tried before that didn't work perhaps would be accomplished effortlessly, without restricted beliefs and therefore with great success.

It's probably best that the majority of us don't become totally new people all at once. It's probably better to evolve gradually, as we retain all of our positive aspects while transforming and overcoming

126

our limited beliefs through the power of the imagination. Albert Einstein said it well: "To imagine is everything!" Every time you go beyond your old beliefs about yourself, you create a new and better you. It's somewhat like looking out a window at a beautiful scene of nature through a dirty glass, then washing it so that it's clear and shining, and then looking out again...the same scene but so much better.

Take some time and really think about who you are. Say your name to yourself, describe yourself. This description tells you more about your past rather than what you could be, right? As the person you've always been, you think the same, have the same reactions, and consequently allow yourself to remain limited, with only a few choices and options which you keep applying and reapplying in all situations, getting the same results. In other words, you keep going in a circle because your self-image was built upon your own imagination - pictures of yourself which grew out of interpretations and evaluations called experiences.

In order to rebuild a positive, attractive self-image,

you need to use the same method that you previously used to build the negative, unattractive self-image. If your imagery is vivid enough and detailed, this imagination practice is equal to an actual experience, insofar as your nervous system is concerned. Isn't that exciting?

You must 'see' yourself as you wish to be, ideally - happy, confident, attractive. It doesn't matter how you were yesterday - and, for now - you needn't have faith that you will be this way tomorrow...if you practice, your nervous system will take care of the 'how'. Just 'see' yourself as you want to be NOW. These exercises build new memories or 'stored data' into your subconscious, that greatest of all computers that will give back to you whatever you put into it.

After practicing for a while, you'll be pleasantly surprised at how you're feeling differently, acting and reacting differently...spontaneously and automatically, without even trying.

If you want to succeed, you need to push *beyond*

those limits that you previously set for yourself.
You've got to do the things you think you can't do!
Tackle the very things you feel are the most difficult
for you. The resistance you feel is that old tug of your
limited beliefs that say you can't...if you give in to
them you're right, you can't. But - tackle them head
on and you will! Robert Kennedy said, "I see
something that's never been and I ask, why not?" And
he was right. WHY NOT? The only thing that holds
you back is your old belief system...change those
beliefs with mental imagery, create a new you! If you
can think it, or imagine it, or feel it...you are already
giving birth to your dream, your goal, at the very time
of the thought. Create that thought and you are
creating a new you. The process begins at that level
of energy! The dream was always there, waiting for
you to clean the windows and 'see' the new you, as
you discover that what you are seeking was always
there, waiting for you to let it out.

YOUR GOAL MONITOR

Review this list often so as to reinforce your progress and correct any inconsistencies. You have learned that natural discipline *and* freedom are both complimentary and mutually rewarding.

*Specific Goal*_____

Date Set _____ *Date Accomplished* _____

*Specific Goal*_____

Date Set _____ *Date Accomplished* _____

*Specific Goal*_____

Date Set _____ *Date Accomplished* _____

*Specific Goal*_____

Date Set _____ *Date Accomplished* _____

*Specific Goal*_____

Date Set _____ *Date Accomplished* _____

Create Yourself...

*Specific Goal*_____

Date Set _____ *Date Accomplished* _____

*Specific Goal*_____

Date Set _____ *Date Accomplished* _____

*Specific Goal*_____

Date Set _____ *Date Accomplished* _____

*Specific Goal*_____

Date Set _____ *Date Accomplished* _____

*Specific Goal*_____

Date Set _____ *Date Accomplished* _____

*Specific Goal*_____

Date Set _____ *Date Accomplished* _____

*Specific Goal*_____

Date Set _____ *Date Accomplished* _____

*Specific Goal*_____

Date Set _____ *Date Accomplished* _____

Create Yourself...

*Specific Goal*_____

Date Set _____ *Date Accomplished* _____

*Specific Goal*_____

Date Set _____ *Date Accomplished* _____

*Specific Goal*_____

Date Set _____ *Date Accomplished* _____

*Specific Goal*_____

Date Set _____ *Date Accomplished* _____

*Specific Goal*_____

Date Set _____ *Date Accomplished* _____

*Specific Goal*_____

Date Set _____ *Date Accomplished* _____

*Specific Goal*_____

Date Set _____ *Date Accomplished* _____

*Specific Goal*_____

Date Set _____ *Date Accomplished* _____

THE TRANSFORMATION!!!

If you want to change your thoughts, your body, your life, and in that order, you need to open up your mind and your heart to the renewal forces within you by using the power of positive thinking and positive meditation, and then exposing yourself to positive people and influences which will help move you towards the positive direction you have chosen.

In the first phase, do not concentrate on trying to change yourself. In trying to concentrate, you'll lose the relaxed attitude that is necessary to elicit positive conditioning. In other words, you need to give the right hemisphere of your brain complete freedom to operate and interact with the left hemisphere as you open the door, so to speak.

For the first three weeks, twenty one days, no less, use a positive statement such as: "I am healthy, I am confident and satisfied!" (You needn't believe it, just say it.) Say this for five minutes at a time, using a watch, ten times daily. There are no side effects and no possible harm to you physically or mentally. Keep a note pad handy and record with a checkmark every time you complete five minutes. Remember, you can be doing other things - driving, taking a shower, whatever, while making your statement. Do this without analyzing for three weeks and then look back...take a good look at yourself. See if you are not more confident, more relaxed, talking and acting in a more positive manner about yourself.

In the second phase, the left hemisphere of your brain will begin to interact with the right hemisphere as you use directed thought processes to help you rewire the circuits in your brain in more positive directions. By using relaxation techniques and positive meditation, along with the conscious conditioning of phase one, you'll get into the habit of making productive, rather than unproductive, inferences about yourself, as well as your environment.

If you're visually oriented you might simply focus on a 'happy' picture, something pertaining to nature that makes you feel good - animals, children, flowers, mountains, a meadow, a lake, the ocean... Or, if you're a more verbal type, read something positive, over and over again - something with a positive message. If you are biblically oriented, choose a positive selection. Some may be drawn to the words of Norman Vincent Peale who said, "Formulate and stamp indelibly on your mind a mental picture of yourself succeeding. Hold this picture tenaciously and never permit it to fade. Your mind will seek to develop this picture. Never think of yourself as failing, and never doubt the reality of the mental image." What Dr. Peale is telling us is to use our imagination.

Your imagination can transform even your physical appearance. Imagine yourself with a beaming, happy face and a radiant personality. Hold this picture in your mind and you will become that kind of person. Visualize yourself as a content, attractive person and your imagination will turn you into exactly that person because you will be guided towards making choices that bring about the transformation.

135

You, and only you, hold the answer in your heart right now. Get your *mental* detector out to detect both positive and negative attitudes, keeping your mental slate as clean as possible of negative thoughts and people. If you are living with a negative person, learn to 'cancel' immediately, any negative statements made by them.

Another warning to pay attention to is if you hear yourself saying, "I've never done that before!" SO WHAT? Don't let that be an excuse for not trying. Do not allow yourself to be intimidated by your own thoughts. (Or others, for that matter.) Positive thinkers - doers - break through the barriers by simply beginning! To begin is half-done. Rembrandt was a beginner once. Every superstar in the big leagues started out as a rookie. Sterilize your negative thoughts (and others) just as you would sterilize an AIDS Virus, because it's even more deadly.

How far would you reach if you knew you could succeed? Open wide the doors of your imagination and let the incredible dreams and hopes flow through.

Now, every time you set a new goal, you have to arrange your priorities. That can be a little rough, but remember the problems are inside your own head - you might have to forego some other goals in order to make this new move. Choose your priorities...and remember to sterilize the negative thoughts that may enter your mind from within or without. Set aside meditation time, every day, protected from uninvited, pressure-producing interruptions. Then begin to use your imagination and visualize.

Visualization is not physical vision, but inner vision. It uses the power of the imagination. Take your mental binoculars and focus on the specific objective that you wish to accomplish. See it! Seize it emotionally and it will be yours!

Now you need to check out your addictions, your private habits - we all have them - we're creatures of habit and this can be used to work for us rather than against us. The point is, are your addictions negative or positive? You need to clean up your act...check your eating habits, your exercise habits, your reading habits, your relaxation habits. I respect your intelligence too much to insult you by telling you what's right and what's wrong. Simply work on eliminating the negative and accentuating the positive...form positive addictions!

And now, it's time for commitment. This is the point of no return because you announce to the world your commitment. It's absolutely amazing how much energy commitment taps and releases to insure your success. A runner may come in last, but if he beats his own record time, he is a success. Everyone has, within him or her the potential for that success, regardless of any handicap, whether it's physical or mental. Your freedom to choose to be successful is the one treasure that no one can ever take from you.

You can change your thoughts, your life, and your body on a daily basis through choices and actions. For most people, the times just after waking up in the morning and before going to sleep are the most creative, open times to retrain and develop your consciousness. How you begin and end your days makes a distinct difference in the quality of how you live your day. I, for example, listen to my own positive, motivational tapes every morning and again at bedtime. This is also a perfect time to repeat the positive statement: "I am filled with Positive Energy," at least ten times. Try it both ways and see the results for yourself. Let yourself wake up grouchy and in a bad mood, with all kinds of negative thoughts and just drift into your day acting and reacting impulsively. Or, wake up to positive programming, and do the same at bedtime as you evaluate your day. Nine out of ten times it will be significantly better, even though the conditions around you are the same. Very often, with continued positive programming, even the conditions themselves begin to change for the better.

You are not avoiding negative thoughts, you are choosing to exclude them from your consciousness, therefore you are in control, not only of your thoughts, but of your life and your body. This is how successful people think - they focus on the goal, consciously *excluding* all that could go wrong to block that goal...they are focused on what could go well. And it works! "A single focus on what could go well instead of badly leads to greater accomplishment in reality."

Success doesn't just happen...it develops, as you develop - just as a flower grows from a seed to full bloom, success grows from a thought by an orderly process of fulfillment. Remember the famous observation of Alice in Wonderland? "It takes all the running that you can do to keep in the same place; if you want to go somewhere else, you must run at least twice as fast as that."

The law of your mind is this: when positive or negative thoughts are conveyed to your subconscious, impressions are made in the neurons or brain cells. As soon as your subconscious accepts an idea, it proceeds to put it into effect and it lines up all the laws of nature to get its way. These are not two minds but merely two spheres of activity within one mind. You think and speak with your conscious mind and whatever you habitually think and say sinks down into your subconscious level, which in turn creates, according to the nature of your thoughts and words.

Your subconscious is the seat of your emotions and is the creative mind. If you think good, good will follow - if you think negative, negative will follow. Again, you can reverse the negative program in your computer by constant conditioning and reinforcement. This reversal process is gradual, taking from three to four weeks, but once you start going forward it's a never ending process. And, once you experience the feeling of overcoming, nothing and nobody can ever knock you down again.

Most important to remember is that once the subconscious accepts an idea, it begins to execute it. The law of your subconscious works for good and bad ideas alike. This law, when applied in a negative way, is the cause of failure and frustration in reaching your goals. However, when your habitual thinking becomes positive, you experience success in all that you undertake.

Whatever you claim mentally as being so, your subconscious will accept and execute into your life. So get your subconscious to accept your positive ideas about you and generate the conditions you desire. You'll have to work on it constantly, because there are always negative factors to overcome. Give the command and the goal is yours.

You may ask, "Can *I* change? Can our brains actually physiologically change?" The answer is YES! YES! YES! Let's say that you're contemplating a major change in your life - you get set to change your course - from negative to positive...what are you up against? What is the biological basis for the behavior or thought patterns that you want to change? New learning entails structural change in the neurons and synapses of the brain. To form a new habit, or make a change, you alter old pathways that gradually weaken and finally disappear, making way for the new, the better.

With a little effort and a lot of practice, it is clear that adults can make changes. It may not be quite as easy as in childhood, but as you acquire new skills and habits and lifestyle, you must practice, practice, practice, obviously in a positive way, with a positive perspective, if you want positive results. The old habits are actively eliminated through the new, positive behavior that modifies old circuits and establishes the alternate pathways in the brain. The adult brain remains extremely flexible into old age. Neurobiologists have shown that we can continue to lay down new synaptic networks well into our eighties or nineties and even beyond, with good nutrition, exercise, and a positive attitude. As human beings we are endowed with a superior ability to learn, to get better and better, even alter our own course in life.

THE WAY YOU ARE...IS NOT NECESSARILY THE WAY YOU WERE

Remember, you are what you think about all day long, so think contentment, peace, and satisfaction within yourself for a *permanently* confident, healthy you. Everything exists first in the mind. Thinking makes it so and thoughts are things. The outer tangibles that appear in our world are the result of the thoughts we have. For example, if you wanted to build a house, you would first think about it. You would *choose* the kind of house you want, how many rooms, etc...then you'd get a set of plans to match your thoughts and next you'd put the plan into action by getting the workmen who would manifest your plan into actual reality. Soon, your house would appear and there you'd be, in your house which would be the result of your thoughts and your imagination.

It's the same with a life. A life is constructed along the lines of one's thoughts...we are the way we are not

144

only because of our parents, but because of the way
we think about ourselves and our lives; what we think
about our world and other people. Since we truly are
what we think about all day long, it makes good sense
to establish guidelines for our thoughts: to be positive,
optimistic, constructive, and enthusiastic in whatever
we think about.

Apparently negative events and/or situations can
leave you feeling helpless, if you allow it. Regardless
of how hopeless a situation may seem, you can always
choose your reaction to it and in so doing, you take
charge of your life and your behavior.

When something happens that catches you
off-guard, your body fills with tension and anxiety;
consequently, you may react with unwanted behaviors
as you respond, either right away or much later,
depending on how deeply you bury it. You can use
these responses as reminders that this particular aspect
of your life needs improving. A positive action is to
change (from negative to positive) your thoughts
regarding something or someone so that positive

development may take place.

Life means change and change means challenges
which can become wonderful opportunities for you.
Your image changes daily because each day's
situations are different, offering you unlimited
possibilities for your growth and evolvement. And,
this is the way it should be. Human beings progress
by change - nature progresses by change: spring,
summer, fall, winter. Can you imagine a tree in
spring if it stubbornly refused to change and bear
leaves? Or, if a rose stubbornly resisted change and
the opportuity to bloom?

Proceed *forward* in this thing called life by
choosing to be the very best that you can be, all of the
time, one moment at a time - the way you want to
look, the way you will be as you put your thoughts in
command. As you begin this exciting program, you
can hitch your wagon of goals and dreams to the star
of faith, joyously *anticipating* glorious new adventures
and challenges. Yes, this is the new you, as you make
this the turning point in your growth and awareness.

146

The past has been but stepping stones to the challenges that lie ahead - *choose* to make this the happiest, healthiest, most fulfilling experience of your life!

Once again, go to your mirror, take a deep breath, look deeply into your eyes and say aloud, *"I am wonderful! I am confident, and healthy, and satisfied in every way."*

And this time, *you really believe it!*